10 Things GREAT Sales Leaders Don't Do!

Avoid These Sales Blunders and Improve Your Performance

DONALD HATTER

10 Things GREAT Sales Leaders Don't Do!

Book Cover design by: Nine Green Studio

Layout by: MELISSA@THEWRITERLAB.COM

Editorial Consultant: Delina Pryce McPhaull

Printed in the United States of America

First Printing, October 2015

ISBN 978-0-9968289-0-1 (sc)

ISBN 978-0-9968289-1-8 (ebook)

BNL Books
PO Box 52326
Houston, TX 77052

For information contact the author at WWW.DONALDHATTER.COM

DEDICATION

In the loving memory of my parents, Fay and Donald Hatter Sr., who paved the way for my success. They challenged me to be the best that I could be while providing love, support and guidance in all of my endeavors.

CONTENTS

INTRODUCTION

There is no shortage of information on how to become a better sales leader. If you Google "sales methods," or "effective sales strategies," or "effective sales techniques" you will find hundreds of millions of results. In addition to what we have access to on the internet and in book stores, most sales leaders have had extensive hands-on training, along with years of experience.

Despite all the sales training materials, sales tools, and sales experience, many sales leaders still struggle with some basic concepts. That struggle leads to behavior which negatively impacts company growth. The recommended ideas and practices you'll find in this book are common knowledge, but not common practice.

The purpose of this book is to identify those thoughts, behaviors, and attitudes that hinder the ability of the sales leader to effectively execute during sales cycles. Most of these activities happen in consultative or strategic selling situations, so you don't see this behavior as much when there is limited to no interaction with the prospect.

This book was written for sales leaders—those who are leading or influencing major sales efforts. A sales leader can be an official member of a sales team (i.e. Account Executive, Sales Manager), or someone that works with the sales team (i.e. General Manager, Product Specialist), or it can be an individual that is now responsible for business development efforts (i.e. a business owner, or a partner at a consulting or law firm).

Based on my experiences, observations, and research, I compiled a list of 10 common sales blunders that great sales leaders avoid. With over 20 years of sales experience that ranges from developing revenue generating partnerships with global brands such Wal*Mart, Shell Oil, ExxonMobil, Texas Instruments, VISA, Johnson & Johnson, and Orascom, to working with small business owners across the United States, these are 10 sales blunders I often see. Making any of these blunders can cause a deal to stall or worse yet, not happen at all. In each chapter you'll find a brief explanation about the behavior that should change, and then I will provide commentary on how the same situations are handled by GREAT sales leaders.

The idea is not to teach the reader another sales methodology, or an entire new set of sales techniques and strategies. The purpose is to point out why an ineffective sales leader should want to alter his or her behavior in a few areas. Depending on your industry, some of the things mentioned will be more relevant than others. For example, if you are a pharmaceutical sales leader trying to increase your sales, the idea of a ROI calculator (Sales Blunder #5) may be irrelevant, and that is ok. No matter what industry you're in, I am confident you will find some insight that will help you close high-dollar transactions faster.

Here's to your success!

SALES BLUNDER #1

Try to Create a Compelling Event

If you are a career sales professional there is a good chance that you have been exposed to one or multiple sales methodologies or trainings. Could be Target Account Selling (TAS), or SPIN selling, or any one of hundreds of others. In many of those methodologies the concept of a compelling event is mentioned. In its most simplistic terms, a compelling event is an event that compels a client or prospect to take an action. For example, it could be a change in regulation that forces the need for changes in the business, or it could be the fact that their current solution may not work after a certain date. The idea taught in these methodologies is that a compelling event needs to exist in order for you to close a deal, or make a sale.

Most salespeople would not disagree with the concept of needing a compelling event to close a deal in a consultative or strategic sales situation; however, many ineffective sales leaders are not able to clearly differentiate between a compelling event and the idea of compelling someone to purchase their solution. The ineffective sales leader may be talented and very knowledgeable about the market and their solution, but that is not enough to compel a prospect to spend if in fact there has been no compelling event. You can't just convince a prospect to spend if they are not ready.

Sometimes a prospect will say things such as "I like your solution better," or "your solution could help us" and the sales leader hears "...we are ready to buy and we want your solution, where do we sign?" Sales leaders are taught that if you remain persistent ultimately you will be able to persuade the prospect to do what you want them to do. In most cases that simply is not true and it leads to wasted sales efforts, and poor forecasting.

There were a couple of occasions early in my career where I believed that I could compel the prospect to spend without a true compelling event. I had a great product, I demonstrated its value as it related to their business needs, I established my credibility with them, and I developed a great relationship with the prospect. I am actually good friends with a couple of these prospects some ten plus years later. Since I developed that friendship I knew that they truly tried to get their management to procure the solution, but it never happened. Our value proposition sounded good to them, but management didn't have solving their problem as a priority. There was no event that compelled them to change their mind, so nothing ever happened.

A compelling event could be something widely known such as a change in regulation, it could also be something that is internal to the prospect and not shared externally. Depending on the complexity of the sale, and the product, you may not ever know what compelled a prospect or client to buy. If you are in a market where you believe a compelling event needs to happen before a prospect or client buys, then you have to know if it has occurred, and you have to realize that you can't create it.

I believe great sales leaders understand that they can't create a compelling event for the prospect. Doing things like reducing your price doesn't create an event that compels them to spend money on your product or solution. If they do buy, it is usually because they have already decided to buy and you just gave them a greater deal. Delivering a fantastic value proposition, showing your pretty slides made by the marketing team, and telling them how much their profit will increase with your solution doesn't create the event either. In fact, with most large corporations the money you are seeking needs to be budgeted and allocated in advance. This can even be true with individuals.

Less effective sales leaders tell other sales professionals all the time that creating a compelling event can be done. They tell others to just keep pushing and setting up meetings and hopefully something will happen. Then they wonder why the close percentages are so low. In many cases when a prospect is enthusiastic about your solution, and it looks like they are going to buy, but then they decide to do nothing, it is because the compelling event was missing. They were not compelled to buy at that time. In industries where sales forecasting is important this becomes an issue. Being able to predict revenue or forecast accurately requires understanding what a compelling event is for the prospect. If you assume you can create one then you will just be guessing about when a deal may close, so the chances of you being correct about your expected revenue is slim.

An important thing to note is that just because a compelling event happens it doesn't mean that the client will buy your solution. In addition, you will not always know when a compelling event is going to happen, so building solid relationships and keeping prospects informed of your products and services is still a value added activity. You want to stay engaged with a prospect so that they call you when the time is right. I just wouldn't forecast a deal or count on completing a sale before I know that a compelling event exists.

Many years ago, I was working for a software company that sold forensic technology which was to be installed on a company's network so that data could be searched and retrieved from all company computers, even down to the hard drives. I was in a group that sold to large corporations vs a group that sold to forensics specialist with law enforcement agencies. I did a number of deals but there was one in particular that I will always remember.

I was actively engaged with a Fortune 500 global technology and specialty materials company. We were having some great conversations and things were progressing. I had developed a good relationship with my primary contact, who understood what we did, and he was interested in purchasing the technology. I thought I was doing a good job of executing on my sales cycle, but they would not commit to buying our solution. There was a great deal of interest, but there was no compelling event. Then surprisingly one day everything changed. My primary contact called me on the Monday of Thanksgiving week. Since there had not been a compelling event over the many months we were engaged, I usually just touched based with him every other week or so. It was unusual to get a call from him unless he was responding to a question I had asked. Nevertheless, I welcomed the call. His interest in our solution had increased tremendously. He wanted me to send him an updated price quote, and he started negotiating before I even had a chance to email the quote. At this point I knew something had happened, so I asked. He hesitantly told me that some employee was found with a file that contained the social security numbers of everyone in the company. Remember, this was a company with thousands of employees all over the globe. The employee was fired, but now my contact had to see if that file existed anywhere else in the company, and that is what our solution did. BAM! That was the compelling event I needed to get the deal closed. The deal was worth roughly $450,000 and we completed it before the end of the week, which wasn't even a full working week because of the holiday.

That was just one example, but the idea is that compelling events are not created by the sales leaders. As in the example above it is good to stay engaged so that when the event happens, the prospect will call you, as my primary contact did. When selling different solutions, and in different industries the compelling event can look very different. For instance, the person stealing social security numbers was pretty drastic. In some other industries, such as selling air conditioning units, the event could be much simpler. Imagine how hard it is trying to sell an air conditioning unit to a household that has a working one. Yes, you can talk about how much more efficient your unit will be, therefore saving them money, and they may or may not buy, but your chances are low. However, imagine how much easier the sale could be if their current air conditioning unit breaks right before you arrive (a compelling event). The homeowner would be much more willing to listen and much more likely to buy.

There may be some exceptions with some products and in some industries. However, great sales leaders realize that if they are selling a product where a prospect needs to be compelled to spend, it is not up to the sales leader to create that circumstance. We have all tried, but we should not be surprised if the sale does not get completed.

GREAT SALES LEADERS

Position themselves to take advantage of a true compelling event.

> "At the start of every stage of the sales process, each opportunity should be assessed to understand the compelling event."
> — **John Kenney**

SALES BLUNDER #2

Over-Estimate Their Value

When dealing with prospects it is important to keep in mind both the company and the individuals you are selling to. How important are your relationships with them? How valuable are you to them?

I have worked with more than one sales leader that has lost perspective and didn't understand how they were viewed by the prospect. Just because they had the title of vice president or general manager they assumed the client would view them as being important, knowledgeable, and therefore valuable.

For example, I once worked for a small software company that sold solutions targeted to large corporate legal departments. Our ideal primary contact would be either the general counsel or assistant general counsel at companies such as Wal*Mart, ExxonMobil, Shell Oil, and other Fortune 500 companies. Our primary targets were companies that spent greater than $20MM a year on outside law firms and other legal service vendors. With most of our target prospects, the general counsel reported directly to the CEO, so they were extremely high on the "corporate food chain." As a result, they were frequently solicited by vendors. Unlike some senior IT managers, the General Counsel and Assistant General Counsel were not in the business of evaluating software vendors. The majority of their time was spent managing legal affairs, and those vendors that help them with legal matters (i.e. law firms).

When selling to those such individuals, telling them that my "VP of Sales is coming to town and he would like to meet with you" was hardly ever effective as a statement by itself. These were high-level executives at literally the largest companies in the WORLD. We were a small to medium size vendor, so the VP title my boss carried meant nothing to them. They were busy and just not that impressed.

Sometimes we would offer to take them to lunch or a baseball game, hoping that the results would be different. They weren't. We figured that meeting during a time like lunchtime, or after work, would not interfere with their daily working hours and that would be better for them. It was worse. If they don't want to speak with you about work during work, then why expect them to want to spend their "free" time talking to you about work? Great sales leaders understand this point very well. Until there is perceived value, meetings are hard to come by with these high-level executives. The title of VP, or a "free" lunch offer simply isn't enough.

In addition, these same individuals received such offers all the time. When you are responsible for spending tens of millions, sometimes hundreds of millions of dollars with over 100 different law firms and other vendors, you can get "free" lunch or "free" baseball game tickets all the time, and from companies where you have already established a relationship.

The prior example was in reference to selling to prospects where it was very early in the sales cycle, but there are also consequences to over-estimating your value further along in the sales cycle.

I was once working with a global software company with headquarters in Australia. The majority of our executive management team moved from Australia to the United States because the potential in the US was greater than in any other part of the globe. Since penetrating the US market was very strategic for us, we raised a lot of money from investors based in California, and subsequently that is where we decided to have our US headquarters office. However, a few of our executives remained in Australia, which is where the company was founded. When executives from Australia came to the US, there was always a big push by our sales leaders to get these executives in front of clients and prospects with the hopes that they would help advance the sales cycle, and potentially increase the size of the deal. On the surface, that thought seemed to make sense because our executives were knowledgeable professionals with great industry experience.

The challenge presented to those account executives in the field (those closest to the prospect) is that sometimes the agenda of our executive wasn't that important to the prospect, so the visit wasn't going to advance the sales cycle. However, it is hard for an account executive to tell his or her boss they add little value at this point in the sales cycle.

On one occasion we had a General Manager (GM) who was in charge of one of our newer products come to the US, and sales leadership required that we set up meetings for her with our "important" prospects. Their explanation was that if we demonstrated the capabilities of this product extension (newer product), it would increase the size of the deal, and help it get to closure faster.

So against my better judgement I complied with our sales leadership and set up a meeting with my biggest prospect at the time. This prospect was a large utility company that just moved slowly in their evaluation, especially when it came to seven figure investments. In addition, moving forward with us required them acknowledging that they "wasted" a lot of money on other attempts to solve the same problem we were going to solve for them. We were far enough along in the process that we were talking about pricing for our core product. They were interested in our solution, but it was a large investment for them, so I didn't think the time was right to talk about increasing that investment by buying software that they could not use any time soon. Nevertheless, I was able to set up the meeting, which was expected to last a couple of hours. They even ordered lunch for the meeting. Most importantly I convinced my point of contact to invite his boss to attend, and his boss controlled the budget.

We prepped our GM by giving her the history of the account, and all the other pertinent details. As a team we were all excited and ready to perform. I was particularly excited because our GM was very intelligent and charismatic, and had sold the core product for years before moving on to be in charge of the new product. So I felt we could talk about the new product for a little bit, but then focus on the product that was more important to them.

So we had the meeting and it turned out to be a disaster! Since we were trying to have several meetings all over the city, we actually showed up late as a result of having a meeting before that was across town. I could not think of another time I had been late for a meeting, especially when it was in the same city in which I lived. Additionally, at some point while our GM was delivering her long-winded presentation on the newer product (the one they didn't need), I realized that the most senior member of their team had literally fallen asleep. Our GM just kept talking. This was another first for me. To top everything off, I was also there with one of my peers who had the GM scheduled to do another meeting immediately after this meeting, so they left early.

So what does all of this mean as it relates to value perception and great sales leadership? My sales vice president had all of the details of the account and knew we had already talked about, and dismissed the need for the newer product. Therefore sending someone in to talk about it again did not add any value as far as the prospect was concerned. This was probably our sixth meeting with the prospect and it was the first time they walked away thinking we had wasted their time. They had six people clear their schedules. They bought lunch. They wanted our core solution. They invited the manager with the money/budget, and we showed up and offered very little value. My vice president of sales was more concerned with giving the GM some interesting meetings to attend than he was with demonstrating value to the prospect. Needless to say that "deal" went sideways from that day on.

Over my career I have been responsible for successfully closing deals with Wal*Mart, Shell Oil, ExxonMobil, Texas Instruments, Waste Management, Orascom E&C, Johnson & Johnson, and many others, so the good news is that you can get to a point where prospects will want to meet with you. It just takes time and you have to show value all along the way. Many times showing value with these larger companies is about working the process and being responsive when needed. Executives can appreciate that you have done that, which is why they put the process in place. Going directly at these executives with inflated titles and agendas that aren't important to them rarely gets the response you are looking for. Great sales leaders gain much more traction by establishing a relationship, concentrating on creating value, and following the process established by the prospect.

With smaller companies similar concepts apply. The way to show value may differ, but the idea of needing to demonstrate value to prospects before asking for things is still the way it works.

Many years ago, I worked with a company where I traveled around the country analyzing small businesses. It was a very different experience than selling to companies like ExxonMobil and Southern California Edison. It was a lot less process oriented and much more emotional. I was there to analyze the business, identify the problems and discuss how much the problems were costing them. After one or two days of analysis, I presented my findings with the goal of having them hire our consultants to start the next day to fix the problems. In complete candor, the analysis wasn't very hard. Many small businesses simply have just different versions of the same problems, so it was easy for me to speak to their problems within the two days.

This market is considerably smaller and has different dynamics so showing value was done differently. They were impressed with my analysis, but that is not what provided them the greatest value. What they were really looking for was someone that understood, appreciated, and cared about how much they worked. Being a small business owner can be challenging, and most of the owners I have worked with were simply overwhelmed. They needed a friend more than anything else.

I literally had more than one owner cry as they asked for help. They were relieved that they found someone that cared and they were happy that help was on the way.

How you add value to a prospect can vary. In the examples above, how to add value was different at Wal*Mart than it was with the owner of a grocery store in rural America. A great sales leader learns the differences and figures out what is best as it relates to their prospects. At the end of the day, everything is best if a true win-win situation is created. But in order to do that you have to add value as an individual, without overestimating the value you bring to the table. People buy from people.

GREAT SALES LEADERS

Understand what the prospect values most and speak directly to it.

"Prospects need to see that you are interested in their business before you can be interesting to them."

– Paul Zengilowski

SALES BLUNDER #3

Spend Time with the "Wrong Prospects"

Who is my best sales leader? Why is he/she so successful?

One can use so many factors when comparing one sales leader to another. The most obvious criteria would probably be the amount of revenue generated, or the number of transactions completed. Perhaps product knowledge or presentation skills is most important for some.

Despite the skill set and knowledge base of a sales leader, I have always thought the biggest difference between a great sales leader and one that wasn't so great, is that the best sales leaders spend the "right" amount of time with the "right" prospects. I realize that it is not always obvious to know in advance who are the "right" prospects because you don't always know who is going to purchase your product or solution without using a crystal ball that works (I never had one that worked). However, the quicker you can separate those that are spending from those that are not, the greater your success will be.

They say that sales is a "numbers game" and that may be true. The thinking is that the more prospects you speak to, the more you will sell, and that seems logical. But in order to speak with more prospects you typically need more time, and your time is limited. That is why it is so crucial to quickly stop pursuing prospects that are consuming your time and resources, but won't be spending anytime soon. This seems like common knowledge, but it is not common practice.

In sales we generally spend a lot of time "qualifying" prospects, which is an integral part of the overall sales process. We develop a set of criteria that we use to help determine if a prospect is worthy of our sales efforts. However, it is important to understand that just because a prospect fits the qualification criteria, it doesn't mean they are your "best" prospects. Too often ineffective sales leaders confuse the concept of "ideal" target with "best prospect."

Over the years I have seen two major reasons why leaders struggle with letting go of the "wrong" prospect.

> ➤ "THEY ARE REALLY IMPORTANT"

In almost every industry, less accomplished sales leaders make the mistake of thinking the "biggest" target is always the "right" prospect to pursue, and therefore all efforts are consumed in that pursuit. Sometimes that is a strategy that works, but it can be dangerous when it doesn't.

Sales leaders and companies figure if they land this "big and strategic" prospect, their business will thrive and everyone will be happy (or something along those lines). That statement is true, but there is an "if" in the middle. This kind of thinking happens not just with account executives and sales leaders, but with companies as well. I have literally seen companies go out of business because they were pursuing their "best" prospect. They allocated the majority of their resources to that one sales cycle and the prospect never spent any money on their solution.

I have been on both "sides of the fence" at different points in my career so I understand why leaders and companies take the risk. There was one point in my career where I was pursuing the world's largest retailer, as well as one of the world's largest oil & gas companies. Acquiring either would have been a huge win for the company, and would lead to us becoming profitable for the first time. I executed on these sales cycles the same as I did with others, but the pressure from the entire management team was a bit more intense. After much effort and careful execution, we signed both companies, which was a huge win for the entire organization. Not only were the deals a nice size, but completing those deals clearly established us as the industry leader.

At another point in my career there were similarly looking "ideal" targets that my manager kept calling our "best" prospects. The situation was similar such that doing a deal with either would have really helped establish our company as an industry leader. However, the difference in this situation versus the other is that both of the organizations had competitive solutions that they were happy with, and they were not changing anytime soon. We had enough conversations with them, and additional insight such that we knew this to be the case. But under the direction of the sales leader I reported to at the time, he could not let it go. He wanted me to call each of them every week. Every now and then we would meet someone new at the company to speak with, but the story was still the same. Needless to say neither spent money with us, and much time and energy was wasted.

The point is that sometimes your "ideal" target is your "best" target and if that is true you should pursue them with vigor. But once you realize that an "ideal" target is not ideal for *you* to pursue, then you should understand that changes need to be made in your strategy. Every hour you spend pursuing a client that is not going to spend is an hour you are not spending pursuing those prospects that may and will spend.

I believe great sales leaders understand the concept so they find out quickly how to spend minimal time with those prospects that are not buying. You may want to spend some time so that you are positioned well in the future to do business, but make it minimal.

➤ "THEY LIKE ME"

Another reason sales leaders get stuck pursuing the "wrong" client is because they have developed a good personal relationship with that client. I use the word personal instead of professional because the prospect isn't buying anything, so that makes it personal. It is almost like the prospect is afraid to tell you no. I think this scenario has happened to all of us at some point in our careers. I know it happened to me.

Sales is a relationship business so we tend to gravitate to those that are nice to us, especially if it is a prospect that appears to meet our qualification criteria. We just figure at some point they will buy from us. After all, they like us and they claim to like our product.

The danger with these kind of relationships is that they are very time consuming, and if the prospect never buys, it is time you should have spent pursuing others.

This situation isn't the same as having a prospect that just takes a long time to make a decision and then eventually buys. We are talking about those prospects that will never buy. Sometimes it can be hard to determine which is which early in the sales cycle, but a great sales leader is good at making that determination. Once the determination is made and you realize the prospect isn't going to buy, there is no reason to be rude, or unfriendly. You just have to make the appropriate adjustments. Stay friendly, but do it at a distance. They will call you if they ever change their mind.

Both scenarios mentioned above can be very enticing for the sales professional because each can generate a lot of activity, and a lot of optimism. The "ideal" prospect represents great potential, and the "friendly" prospect represents an "easy" sale, so it is not hard to see why there is such optimism. As a sales leader, you can't let the optimism take over your better judgement. These situations can become very toxic if you are not careful.

Great sales leaders clearly understand that time is their most valuable asset and how they spend it impacts their success. Sales is a numbers game and activity is extremely important. It is impossible to generate sales without it, but it is the quality of the activity that is most important. If you take a look at an average sales team, rarely is the best producer the person with the most activity.

Making the determination between the "right" and "wrong" prospects is not always easy. As sales professionals it is in our nature to believe we can convince any desired prospect to say "yes". We believe we can make the "ideal" prospect the "right" prospect. We say things like "…objections are not bad, now that we know them we can overcome them." It is in our nature to never give up. Generally speaking those are all good traits to have. However, the earlier in a sales cycle you can identify that a sale is not going to happen, the better off you are. This is why your most successful sales leaders can get away with having less activity than their counterparts who are less successful. The great sales leader spends a higher percentage of their time with prospects that turn into clients.

GREAT SALES LEADERS

Spend the majority of their sales efforts with the "right"
prospects, and intuitively know, early-on, which
prospects are not worth pursuing.

---

*"I prefer to work with those prospects that are
looking for a solution to buy."*

– Donald Hatter

SALES BLUNDER #4

Ignore the Real Problem

I have been told that most good pet stores will not sell you fish at the same time you buy a new fish tank. However, an impatient customer has options and will often purchase the tank at one place and then go somewhere else to buy the fish. Then they take both the fish and the tank home, fill the tank, put the fish in the water immediately, and realize that the fish will be floating at the top of water the next day. Were the fish defective or was it the water to blame for the death of the fish?

The sales environment is much like this scenario.

The reason fish were floating the next day was because the water (environment) was not properly prepared. It takes some time and the right preparation to ensure the environment/water is ready, which is why the good pet stores do not want to sell the fish at the same time as the tank. They do not want you to make the mistake of putting the fish in the tank before it is ready. They prefer for you to buy the tank, fill it, treat the water correctly, and then go get the fish to put in the tank once the water is ready.

Who is to blame if the sales team is struggling? Is it the sales leader, or the individual sales professional?

In situations where we see sales leaders with turnover as high as 100% or 200%, I am inclined to believe that the fish were not defective, so to speak. In those types of situations the common denominator is the sales leader and the environment that he or she has created. It can't always be everybody else's fault.

I once worked for a VP of Sales who hired 14 account executives to fill and refill 5 direct report positions in less than 2 years. It was amazing especially considering it took about 6-9 months to bring an Account Executive up to speed. I just saw people come and go. Many quit and some got fired. In my opinion some were more talented than others, but most seemed like great sales professionals. Some I could not tell because their tenure was way too short to be able make a determination. So, was the problem the fish (14 different account executives), or the water (the sales VP and the environment he created)? I think the answer is simple, but surprisingly, companies struggle with that question. Even if the skill sets of the account executives were not great, they still were all hired by that same VP. Isn't building a team part of the responsibility of the sales leader? The sales leader is also responsible for personal development, retention, and the environment as a whole.

Typically the turnover percentage is higher for less established companies than it would be with older and more established companies, and that seems to be consistent with the thought that it is the water/environment instead of the salespeople. More established companies work hard to create an environment conducive to employee productivity because they understand it is needed for the company to be successful.

Great sales leaders are often true leaders who are very good at hiring, training and mentoring their team, which can lead directly to lower turnover and higher productivity. They are not afraid to take blame for the environment they have created which is the first step in fixing problems.

This problem is not isolated to corporations. I saw the same issue when consulting with small business owners. Most of them came up with two reasons/excuses for not achieving the results they desired. "I just need to sell more, and I need better employees" was something I heard over and over again. I pointed to McDonald's and Wal*Mart as examples of companies that have figured out how to make inexperienced workers productive. They both have spent a considerable amount of time establishing policies and procedures which creates an environment for all to be successful, regardless of skill set.

Great sales leaders understand that hiring quality talent is important, but creating an atmosphere in which all employees can be successful is even more important. Chances are most (not all) account executives will be successful if the company provides them with a clear vision, properly defined goals, easy to understand procedures, and great sales leadership. If those things don't exist, is it really their fault that they are not successful?

GREAT SALES LEADERS

Focus on solving problems and not assigning blame.

"The right people, well-prepared, can inspire change and turn around bad numbers."
– William L. Minx

Sales Blunder #5

Rely Heavily on ROI Calculators

In many industries, organizations will equip their salesforce with a sales tool called a Return on Investment (ROI) calculator. The calculator could be a sophisticated application that took months to develop, or it could be as simple as a spreadsheet that requires only a couple of data points. The idea is that a sales professional will use this wonderful tool to show the prospect what kind of return they will see once they make an investment in whatever solution is being sold. This is certainly a very common occurrence in industries that sell products where determining unique business value and measurable business outcome is harder to do (i.e. the software industry). Not sure you need such a tool if you are talking about selling cell phones.

Companies can spend a lot of time and money developing such tools, and sales professionals spend a lot of time trying to figure out the best way to use the tool with clients and prospects. Conventional wisdom is that once the prospect sees the return on their would-be investment, they will have all the justification they need to move forward and purchase the proposed solution. If you can prove to them that they will get back $300 for every $100 they spend with you, why would they not move forward? Not only have you "justified" the purchase, but you have also provided them with "proof" from this "objective" tool. The tools themselves may even give a short term boost of confidence to the sales professional because the returns always look great.

Over the course of my career I have used a few different types of ROI calculators varying in complexity, but there was one calculator that really stood out. I was working for a Vice President who really believed in the power of the ROI calculator as a sales tool, so he actually hired a consulting firm to have one built. The firm was small, but projects like these were their specialty. They took time to come up to speed on the industry and our solution which was admirable. After a few months, and several iterations they produced a tool that simply looked outstanding. It was presented to the sales team and once we saw it we were all excited and ready to go close deals! Not only did we believe we could close deals, but we also believed we had justification for increasing our price on deals.

On the surface, the ROI calculator seems like a very useful tool; however, there a few limitations that great sales leaders realize.

> ➢ IT DOESN'T REALLY HELP IN COMPETITIVE SITUATIONS: It is not hard to put together a ROI calculator which produces great results. This is true whether you are simply using a spreadsheet, or you

have invested in a more sophisticated tool. Therefore, you and each of your competitors can produce impressive looking results from a ROI calculator. So in a competitive situation there usually is no advantage to using the calculator, since in theory, all solutions would produce results that show great returns.

➤ IT DOESN'T ADDRESS THE CURRENT SITUATION ADEQUATELY: By definition, ROI calculators talk about what happens once a client spends money (makes the investment), and that is actually just a prediction of what could happen. There is no guarantee your predictions will be correct. However, with that being said, most companies decide to make investments based on what happens if they don't spend, or if they allocate the funds to something else. Seems like a subtle difference, but it is an important difference nonetheless. So for example, if you tell a prospect that if they spend $10 on your solution, they will realize a $20 savings, which sounds good! I mean that is a 2 to 1 return. However, if some other vendor working with that company solving a completely different problem delivers a ROI scenario where a $10 investment will lead to $40 in savings then your proposal doesn't look as good as you think. Since the other solution is solving a different problem, you probably will never even find out about the other solution. This happens a lot with IT projects and solutions. The CIO is ultimately making company-wide decisions, so they are prioritizing projects across a number of business owners. Therefore the data you are giving them about your solution could be just a small part of the overall picture.

> ➤ THE CALCULATOR ALONE DOESN'T MAKE A COMPLETE BUSINESS CASE: Every time a prospect is presented the results from a ROI calculator, I believe they become numb to the projected returns. They just assume if you have a ROI tool that it will not be hard to show great returns. In addition, there are other parts of the business case that the tool just assumes are not a risk, so they are not addressed at all. For example, a client wants to be confident in your ability to deliver your product or service. This is vital in their assessment of your perceived value, but it isn't something that is adequately addressed in the ROI tool.

I have seen leaders who believe you can justify a premium price based on a ROI calculator. I believe a great sales leader realizes that you can't justify a price, or even win a deal because of a ROI calculator.

The ROI calculator can be a tool that is helpful in engaging the customer, but it doesn't differentiate your solution in most cases. That was the situation with the example I mentioned above. In sales cycles where I had established a good relationship with the prospect, we held meetings to go over the tool. I collected data, entered it into the tool, and we produced nice looking results. The prospects were impressed, temporarily that is. It never was a reason for why we closed the deal. I believe one prospect that became a client used the results from the tool as one of her exhibits for the business case she had to present. That was probably the most use we received from all of our efforts with the tool.

Great sales leaders realize that there is limited value in tools that don't provide competitive advantages, or truly demonstrate unique business value, and therefore they don't see a huge value in ROI calculators.

GREAT SALES LEADERS

Focus on tools that provide a competitive advantage.

"Focus on demonstrating unique business value that disrupts the status quo."
– Tony Frazier

SALES BLUNDER #6

Assume that the Prospect Can't See

Recently I received an email from a vendor where the first line said "I have sent you several emails in the past...."

I saw this on my smartphone without having to open up the email. I was able to see the name of the sender and because the name didn't ring a bell, obviously I had chosen to ignore them in the past. I likewise deleted this email. The sales leader apparently thought I could not see, because there really was no need to send me the same email several times.

Nowadays it is likely that a recipient will actually see and/or read the email. Before all executives had smart phones they often would have their administrators or executive assistants read and monitor their emails, so there was a chance the person you wanted to see your message never did. That practice is less likely today. People now look at their phones all day. They can be in meetings, on conference calls, or even watching their child's dance recital and they will be scanning their phone.

If you are a sales leader and your prospect has not responded, here are a few reasons why you may not have heard back from them, all of which have nothing to do with whether or not they SAW your messages.

> ➢ NO VALUE IN THE EMAIL: In the example I mentioned above, a great sales leader would have understood that I did not respond to any of the first few messages because I saw nothing of value in them. It doesn't mean that it wasn't well written, or there were errors in it such as bad grammar or misspellings. It also doesn't mean that I received so many emails that I never saw it. In complete candor, I could not remember the first few emails from that vendor, and I didn't open up that latest email. Once I saw the first line of the vendor's last email I realized there was not a need to even open it up. I assumed that the latest email would be just as non-valuable as the previous messages. The point here is that great sales leaders are careful with every piece of communication between a prospect and themselves. They understand that every message should have some substance that the prospect cares about.

> ➢ THEY DO NOT HAVE INFORMATION YOU WANT TO HEAR: It is rare that a client has some great information for you and they have not responded to your attempts to reach them. So continuing to send them emails asking for great news is not a good idea, and great sales managers understand that. There is no need to send an email saying something like "...I have not heard from you but I am wondering if you have

decided to buy our product yet?" Rarely, if ever, will the answer to that be YES, so don't send the email. There is an old saying that says people don't like to be sold to, but they like to buy. If a prospect is ready to buy they will call you, or at the very least, return an email.

➢ THE PROSPECT RECOGNIZES IT IS A GENERIC EMAIL: When sales professionals send me emails and my name is not at the top of the email I rarely read the content. So if the email is not addressed to me by name, I just assume there is a good chance it has no value to me either. That is just an assumption that I make, which could occasionally be wrong. However, the sender doesn't get a response. Most prospects just assume that generic emails are SPAM.

➢ YOU HAVE THE RIGHT CONTENT, BUT SENT IT TO THE WRONG PERSON: Sometimes emails are well written and they do contain content that would be valuable for the company, but they are sent to the wrong person within the company. We would like to think that if that is the case that the person receiving the email will forward it to the appropriate person. In an ideal world that would happen. Unfortunately, we don't live in an ideal world. In a large company the person incorrectly receiving the email may not even know the person it is addressed to. Imagine that you work in the marketing department, and you get a well written email that mentions the benefits of implementing a new payroll system. There is a good chance that message never gets delivered to the right person.

➢ IT COULD HAVE GONE INTO A SPAM FOLDER: If you are not sending generic emails this should not happen. Therefore this is probably the most unlikely reason someone would not respond to your email.

Those are all valid reasons why you may not get a return response from a prospect. Great sales leaders realize that their clients and prospects can see, and therefore they don't keep sending multiple emails with the same content.

To increase your chances of getting a response, each email should be addressed to a particular person, and contain content that is valuable to that particular recipient. Those two factors will not guarantee a response, but it improves your chances. I know that seems self-explanatory, but make sure you keep that in mind next time you get ready to cut and paste content from one email to another.

GREAT SALES LEADERS

Ensure there is perceived value to the prospect with every interaction (email, phone, meeting).

> *"Prospects can see emails that have value to them."*
>
> **– Donald Hatter**

SALES BLUNDER #7

Believe the Prospect Cares About Their Urgency

Almost every sales leader has his or her goals defined based on some accomplishments that need to be achieved by a certain date or time. Depending on the size of the solution you are selling, this date could be the end of the day, week, month, quarter, or fiscal year. As these deadlines approach and you haven't accomplished your goals, the pressure starts to mount. As annoying as that may be, sales professionals all understand that it is part of the job.

Even though it is understood that this pressure comes with the job, I still see sales leaders believe that their urgency automatically translates into urgency for the prospect. That assumption rarely represents reality, and when it doesn't I have seen sales leaders make some strategic selling mistakes. If the prospect truly isn't in a position to buy, then I would not try to convince them to change their mind by doing any of the following things:

> **DROP THE PRICE:** This is a mistake I see all the time. If a prospect is not in position to buy, a price reduction doesn't change things. For example, if they have to go through a procurement process that can't be completed before your deadline, then decreasing the price will not help. Or if they are at a point where they do not have the approval, the decrease in price might make your solution look more desirable, but it doesn't get your deal done before the deadline. The major problem with dropping the price however, is that you have lowered the price without getting anything in return. If you lower the price in order to get them to complete the sale now and they can't complete the sale until later, they are still going to want the lower price that you offered when you were under pressure. If you are selling a high-dollar item or service this is almost always true. If you are selling a low-dollar item, the prospect may decide not to buy at all. Think about your own buying behavior. Let's say that you see something you want to purchase and it is 50% off this week, but for whatever reason you can't buy until next week. What happens when you go to buy the product next week and it is full price? Chances are you will either wait until it is on sale again, or not buy it at all.

> **CONSTANTLY CALL:** If you have developed a relationship and the prospect understands your product, there is no need to call every day. The daily phone call or email rarely, if ever, creates urgency for the prospect. More often than not, they will just become annoyed.

> **CIRCUMVENT A PROCESS:** If the prospect has a process that needs to be followed, then be diligent and

complete the process as quickly as possible. Don't try to cut corners because that will only hurt you in the long run. I learned this the hard way. I was once in a situation where I got the prospect to give the go-ahead by the desired deadline, but since all of the steps required by procurement were not followed, the paperwork could not be completed, which meant the sale could not be finalized by the desired date. Ultimately my point of contact wasn't clear on the process, and since he was very senior in the organization I never thought to verify if he understood it. From that day forward, I vowed to ask questions to verify that the prospect and I both knew the process.

> **GIVE AWAY YOUR LEVERAGE:** Perhaps the prospect is ready to buy before your deadline, which is great. It could be a situation where they can buy, but it is not urgent for them. So they could buy now, or they could buy later. In this situation it is ok, to provide small incentives if that is needed to complete your sale before your deadline. However, you don't want to create a "bad" deal by giving too much of an incentive, or by giving the wrong incentives. So if you are negotiating, don't turn a position of strength into a position of weakness because you're under pressure.

Great sales leaders understand that pressure put on them does not constitute pressure for the prospect. No matter how good or bad you are as a sales leader there will always be times where you are trying to get business transactions completed near a deadline, but here are some ways that great sales leaders go about getting those deals completed before their deadlines:

> **DEVELOP A GREAT RELATIONSHIP WITH THE PROSPECT:** The better your relationship is with a prospect the better your chances are of getting the

prospect to help you out. If they can't help you then at a minimum you can get a candid answer as to what is actually possible.

➢ DILIGENT ABOUT THE PROCESS: If there is a procurement process, be very diligent about following it. Don't put yourself in a position where you have missed something.

➢ ACT WITH URGENCY THROUGHOUT THE PROCESS: Assume that your deadline is earlier then it is and act accordingly. If you act with a sense of urgency throughout the process, you and the prospect will find that you get things done quicker and there is no need for a last minute push.

➢ INCREASE THEIR URGENCY: Yes, I mentioned earlier that you can't transfer your urgency and make it theirs, but you can give them reasons why they want to move faster. For example, pick an event that is important to them and work backwards. If a prospect is buying something that needs to be built, delivered, or implemented, and they want it by a certain date, then you can use that information. Help them understand to ensure that is possible they must do things on the timeframe you are suggesting. And of course, you suggest a timeframe that works for you and your deadline.

GREAT SALES LEADERS

Create urgency on the client's side in order
to get deals done faster.

> *"Unless you have created tremendous equity from past business relationships, the prospect will not have empathy for your business urgency. The prospect's loyalty is to their ultimate boss. Unless both interests align and there is a shared benefit, there is no urgency."*
> **– Dr. Richard Brooks**

SALES BLUNDER #8

Let Others Control Meetings

Sales leaders involved with complex sales quickly figure out that being able to obtain and conduct quality meetings has a huge impact on their success. Sales is about building quality relationships, and you have to meet with prospects to build those relationships. Depending on your industry, and your company's brand recognition, quality meetings can be costly to obtain. For companies without good brand recognition, the process can be very daunting. Figuring out who the "right" people are is one process, and then convincing them to meet with you in person is another process. Prospects are busy and they value their time, so they need the right incentive to schedule time with you.

Assuming it all works and you are able to get your desired audience to meet you, there are some things that need to happen prior to, during, and after the meeting if you plan to be successful.

Early in my career, this happened to me. I would always be prepared and excited to be attending the meeting with prospects that represented great potential, but I would let my primary contact control the meeting. They would make the introductions, go over the agenda, and do most of the talking. I just figured I would speak when needed and everything would be ok. It seemed like a reasonable thing to do. What I didn't realize was that by being somewhat passive I couldn't build my credibility in the same way I could if I took control and established myself as the expert on the subject. I also couldn't set the expectation that I was in control of the process, which becomes important in long sales cycles.

I believe that as soon as the meeting is scheduled, great sales leaders realize that it is now *their* meeting and they take control. You can never guarantee that there will always be a fit, or an immediate need for an additional meeting, but here are a few additional things I have seen great sales leaders do to increase their chances of being successful:

> ➢ DRAFT AGENDA: Send a draft agenda prior to the meeting (depending on your business this could be done verbally). This does three things: 1) It is the start of you controlling the format and content of the meeting 2) It shows that you are organized, and that you are preparing 3) If there are any objections to what you want to do, the prospect will tell you in advance of the meeting.

> ➢ SHOW UP EARLY BUT NOT TOO EARLY: Great sales leaders do not show up late, especially if there is prep required for the meeting. They will have hammered out any issues (i.e. projector problems)

before the scheduled start of the meeting. However, they also don't show up too early. Seems subtle but showing up too early (i.e. 45 minutes before a meeting) can be a little annoying for the prospect if they were trying to finish some other task before your meeting.

➤ COMMAND THE ROOM: It should be clear who is leading the meeting. There are a number of ways to do this, and it is primarily based on your personality. Some leaders can simply do it by the strength of their voice. Some always make sure that they are standing while speaking. The trick is not to be obnoxious, while at the same time not blending in.

➤ CONTROL THE PACE/TIME: Sending the draft agenda in advance, and then getting people to agree on an agenda at the beginning of the meeting will help. Also at the beginning of the meeting you should ask/confirm the length of the meeting, and then state *"that is enough time for us to cover what we need"*. That statement is just another subtlety that gives the prospect more confidence in your ability to make the best use of their time. As the meeting continues, always be aware of the time. Don't be one of those people that finds out there are five minutes left in the meeting and then rushes to cram in 25 minutes of presentation into those five minutes. That never works well and it makes you look bad, and then you usually don't get to adequately talk about next steps. Always be prepared to wrap up the meeting on time, and if they want to extend it, that is ok.

➤ BE INTERESTING: It is hard to explain how to do this, and it just comes naturally for many. I don't recommend trying to be a comedian, or doing something weird and out of your comfort zone. Just realize this could be to your competitive advantage.

People may not buy from you just because you are interesting, but they are much more inclined to meet with you again.

Meetings are an important part of the consultative selling process. Prospects only have a limited amount of time and they are usually meeting with multiple vendors. Having an outstanding solution and reputation are crucial, but that combination by itself is not always the deciding factor. Great sales leaders realize that the company brand and your personal brand are not necessarily the same. They also never forget that people buy from people.

Great sales leaders use meetings as a sales tool. They see it as more than a way to talk about how their solution is a great match for your problems. They also use meetings as a way to show competence and enthusiasm, while building credibility with the prospect. Little things like showing up early and commanding the room show enthusiasm. Creating the agenda and being diligent about time helps with your credibility. It shows that you are able to do what you say you'll do in the amount of time allocated, and therefore they will feel more comfortable about giving you more time. Great sales leaders never forget that it's as much about building relationships as it is about the actual solution.

GREAT SALES LEADERS

Take control of meetings and use them to
enhance their credibility.

---

*"Successful salespeople provide an agenda
before the meeting and ask for feedback in
the beginning. Great meetings end with action
items being divided between prospect and
vendor."*

– George Eggert

SALES BLUNDER #9

Misrepresent the Competitive Landscape

We all spend a lot of time and resources trying to figure out what our competitors are doing. Depending on the size of the company, it is not uncommon for a person to be responsible for gathering and disseminating competitive intelligence. It is assumed having this knowledge will help the company better define the uniqueness of its offering, which will help in its sales efforts.

However, commenting on competitors in front of a prospect can lead you down a slippery slope. The reality is that it is easier for the prospect (who is the potential buyer) to get much more accurate information about your competitors than you. So more often than not, if the prospects ask you, "how are you different than your competitors?" they already have more information than you do.

So how might the less effective sales leader respond to the question?

> *"Our product can do this and that and we are the only one that can."*
> *"The work that the other companies provide is simply not as good."*
> *"We are the best, I can provide a list of references."*
> *"We are cheaper so it is a much better deal."*

Those are just a few of the common responses. There are a couple of problems with those answers. The first is that in most industries it is hard, sometimes impossible to know who all of the competitors are, let alone what all they offer. So when you start commenting on what a competitor doesn't have, or what they can't do, you might just be wrong. Things are constantly changing. Last time you checked they might not have had "xyz" or might not have been able to do "xyz", but now they do.

Companies may assign someone to keep everyone current, but not everything competitors are doing is public knowledge. In fact, companies usually share ideas or actually test products with prospects before they become ready to introduce to the market as a whole. This just highlights the chances that you will speak incorrectly if you assume you know the latest about all of your competitors.

When doing consultative selling, it is important to build trust and credibility with the prospect, and being wrong about things is a quick way to lose both. Just think about the times you are a buyer and you are consulting with a salesperson and they say something that you know is wrong. What happens? You start to look at them differently, because they are using inaccurate information to justify why you should spend with them. You don't know if they are accidently giving you inaccurate information, or if they are trying to be sneaky. Neither reason is beneficial to the salesperson.

Providing references may sound ok, but it doesn't really differentiate your offering in any detail. It merely suggests that the people receiving your product or service were happy with it. That is why references typically aren't checked until after a decision to move forward with your solution has been made.

Unless you are selling a commodity you certainly don't want to start with saying your prices are cheaper. You want the prospect to concentrate on overall value, not price. In addition, the price is the easiest thing for a competitor to change without you knowing.

So how might a great sales leader respond to the question "...how do you differ from your competitors?"

"I am not exactly sure, because I have not seen or used anyone's solution. Assuming you have evaluated a few, please tell me what you have liked, and what you didn't like? "

I have used that response often and it works well for a few reasons. First, you don't lose credibility by offering up outdated or inaccurate information. Second, and perhaps more importantly, the prospect answers the question and takes you to a point in the conversation where you want to go. It is great when they start telling you exactly what is most important to them. So instead of simply regurgitating some information that the marketing team put together on competitors, you get to describe your uniqueness in a more meaningful way. No matter what their answers are, you now have data you can work with.

So there is value in knowing about competition. The knowledge you gain can be used during your sales cycle if the information is accurate. Knowing what your competitor has to offer can better help you position your offering, which increases your chances of closing a deal or making a sale. However, it is always safe to assume you don't know all of the competitors along with all of their capabilities.

GREAT SALES LEADERS

Turn the focus of the conversation with a prospect to what they are doing, instead of what the competition is doing.

> *"Educated prospects probably know more about the competitive landscape then any one particular vendor."*
>
> **– Sam Ford**

SALES BLUNDER #10

Misunderstand Their Leverage in a Sales Cycle

No matter what you are selling you never want to negotiate from a point of weakness. Understanding the leverage you have is very important when it comes to negotiating good deals for you and your company. Great sales leaders understand the leverage they have, and they become strategic about using it correctly. In situations where they have little or no leverage, they understand that they need to get some or increase it before negotiating.

Here are a few of the problems that can happen when you don't understand your leverage, or lack of:

> ➢ You try to close too early:
> ➢ You negotiate bad deals:

You try to close too early

Closing too early creates problems, and it is not the same as a "trial" close. A trial close is when you "test the waters" with a client to see how much work you have to do in the sales cycle. You are typically asking open ended questions that allow the client to respond in a way that gives you more information about what you still need to do. For example, you may say something to the effect "...based on what you have heard so far, what do you think? What do you like best about our offering?" A trial close can be an effective sales strategy, whereas closing too early is not a good sales strategy.

"Closing too early" is the same as saying you are trying to close before you have created enough perceived value for the prospect. This perceived value is your leverage and it needs to be created before you start negotiating details. In industries where you are not selling a commodity, this is one reason why salespeople don't want to mention price too early. If the prospect sees what may appear to be an expensive price before they see value in what you are proposing, they will likely just tell you, "no thanks." If they are nice they may say, "I like your product or solution but it is too expensive." This gives you a chance to go back and build value. However, if you close too early there is a good chance the prospect will keep the conversation limited because they don't want you to try again.

As individual consumers, we probably have all had experiences where someone tried to sell us something and they gave us the pricing before we even know what it was exactly they were offering. Those situations never turn out well for the sales professional. If it is someone on the phone, we usually just say, "no, thank you" and hang up. If it is someone at our door, we say no thank you, smile, and then close the door. You get the idea.

Having a true understanding of your leverage means you have a good idea of how much perceived value you have, or have not created, therefore you will know when to close. Great sales leaders generally have a good gauge on how much leverage they have created and they use it appropriately. If they don't have enough they develop strategies to get more.

YOU NEGOTIATE BAD DEALS

In situations where you are confident the prospect is going to buy your product or solution, it is still important to understand your leverage so that you can ensure completion of the sale, and so that you can create better deals for you and your company.

You can do a number of things to increase your leverage. However, if you are not careful, some actions can decrease your leverage. Here are just a couple of ways that I have seen poor sales leaders give away their leverage:

> ➢ ACTING TOO ANXIOUS – When ineffective sales leaders get to the point where they are finally on the verge of landing that "BIG and strategic" client, their initial reaction is pure excitement, which is fine. But then the negotiation starts and if it is not going smoothly, the fear that the deal may fall apart creates anxiety causing the inexperienced sales leader to panic. Panic is never good for keeping your leverage. When you panic, you tend to make unnecessary concessions because you ignore what leverage you have.

> ➢ FEAR OF THE DEADLINE – If you have been selling long enough, you understand the pressure of needing to close business before the end of the day, end of the quarter, or end of the fiscal year. How you approach this situation with the prospect can be a delicate situation. I have seen sales leaders make concessions,

hoping the prospect would sign before the deadline, and that can be dangerous. For example, I have seen companies over-promise on their ability to deliver the solution. They do this by making a promise to deliver quicker than they actually can, or sometimes they will make a promise to deliver more than they actually have. Both situations are bad for long term success, and both of these situations happen when we sales leaders are trying to close without having the appropriate leverage.

All throughout my career, understanding leverage, how to create it, and how to use it has been very important for creating win-win situations and developing great long-term relationships. There is one sales cycle in particular where these concepts could not have been truer.

We were a small software company trying to grow and dominate our market sector, and in this instance, we were literally selling to one of the largest companies in the world. At the time they were either first or second on the Fortune 500 list, so you can imagine how big of a strategic win it represented for us. We targeted mainly Fortune 500 companies, but this prospect was different. They had a reputation of understanding their leverage and using it to get the best possible prices from all of their vendors. They took pride in that reputation because they say that is how they are able to offer their customers such low prices.

Not surprisingly every one of our competitors had been targeting this particular prospect for years.

Now that a compelling event had happened and it became clear they were in the market for a solution, you can imagine how the pressure to complete a deal with them intensified.

Everyone on our management team was now very interested in this particular sales cycle.

They were targeted by every vendor in our industry, but when the evaluation got serious they had narrowed down their search to three vendors. Out of the three vendors, we started in second place, but after a few meetings we became the vendor of choice. At some point shortly after we became the vendor of choice, they wanted to talk about pricing. Well, what they really wanted was to get us so excited with the possibility of doing business with them that we would move closer to drastically reducing our price for our solution. After all, that was their reputation, and they didn't deny it.

Shortly after we were selected, the IT manager from the prospect set up a phone call to discuss pricing and next steps. She included all the decision makers. As you can imagine we were excited. To have all the decision makers on one call from a company that large is a rare occurrence. At some point in the call, pricing came up, and she was upset that it wasn't much less. There literally was a part of the call that was very contentious. The IT manager was essentially trying to beat us up on price and I wasn't interested in taking a beating, especially not this early in the procurement process. I knew we had enough leverage that we could delay finalizing the price. Even though pricing was critically important, I knew they wanted to do business with us. I had developed a great relationship with the prospect, and I was confident we had a solid product. My boss on the other hand, was much more nervous. When he heard the contention he was very concerned, and after the call he let me know in some not so pleasant terms. I told him to relax. We were going to get this deal, we just needed to let it play out. We had leverage, and I had a plan to increase our leverage.

Fortunately for me, I understood that their procurement process was long and extensive. So I suggested that we delay the pricing conversation for a bit and focus on the other parts of the procurement process. To them price is most important, but I said, "let's make sure everything else is also taken care of because if not, price will not matter." It took a little convincing, but the IT manager believed that made sense, so she agreed. My thinking was that the further we moved down the procurement process, the more my leverage would increase. After all, they didn't want to go through the process and then have to choose another vendor and go through it again.

After we had progressed through the procurement process, I requested a meeting where we could address, and hopefully agree on a price. I said I would have the authority to agree on a final price from our side and I requested they had someone on their side that could do the same. At this point in the process my leverage had increased, and I was ready. Needless to say we had the meeting and came to an agreement on price in less than 30 minutes! I was amazed and extremely excited! Not everyone on their side was as happy because they thought I/we got the better deal, and this was a very unusual experience for them. They were so used to beating up on vendors, but in this case it was a fair deal. I understood our leverage and I turned it into a HUGE win for the company. Since they were such an important strategic win for us, my CFO had given me the ability in advance to reduce our price another 40%, but fortunately I didn't have to do that. I knew we had the leverage and I used it to our benefit. I knew they wanted to procure our services and we had completed all the other parts of their complicated procurement process. Understanding and using your leverage is such an important part of being a great sales leader.

Companies, and individual sales leaders can sink or swim based on their ability to harness their leverage.

GREAT SALES LEADERS

Understand their leverage in a sales cycle and they work to increase it before negotiating.

"Until the prospect's pain point has been revealed, there is no leverage. Leverage only comes when a meaningful solution has been communicated which addresses an immediate and potentially costly pain point. "
– Dr. Richard Brooks

ABOUT THE AUTHOR

Donald Hatter is a sales and marketing professional with more than 20 years of professional experience developing partnerships with global brands such as Wal-Mart, Shell Oil, American Airlines, ExxonMobil, Texas Instruments, Waste Management, Halliburton, Johnson & Johnson, and Visa. He also lends his expertise to innovative startups, mid-sized companies and regional organizations who seek him out for consulting, marketing leadership, training events and conferences.

He holds a Bachelor of Arts in economics from the University of Pennsylvania, where he was a member of the varsity football and varsity track & field teams. He also earned a Masters of Business Administration with a concentration in marketing from the University of Pittsburgh's Katz Graduate School of Business.

WWW.DONALDHATTER.COM